# Selected Poems

IAN McMILLAN

*Selected Poems*

First published in 1987 by
Carcanet Press Limited
Conavon Court
12-16 Blackfriars Street
Manchester M3 5BQ

Copyright © Ian McMillan 1987

**British Library Cataloguing in Publication Data**

McMillan, Ian, *1956-*
    Selected poems. —— (Poetry signatures)
    I. Title
    821'.914            PR6063.A2537/

    ISBN 0-85635-718-9

The publisher acknowledges the financial assistance
of the Arts Council of Great Britain.

Typeset in 10pt Palatino by Bryan Williamson, Manchester
Printed in England by SRP Ltd, Exeter

# Contents

from *How the Hornpipe Failed* (1984)

from *Six* (1985)

*Tall in the Saddle* (1986)

## Signs and Wonders

It is almost too good to be real
on this Advent Sunday and Blake's birthday.

Thunder rocking our crisp air.

Children as in a print of children
swing under the tree that is always here.

> A cloud shaped like a fist
> with a finger pointing

> A light, noiseless
> scanning across the sky

Too false          Too explicit

I can plumb a joke about it in the car;
a weak line about headless horsemen.
The others notice
a small woman scuttling across the road.

Bill detects it, in church.
We do something wrong, simple;
he looks up and points
    "The roof'll fall in."
Wince.

However the signs are signs of nothing,
a few small triumphs, disasters, blisters.
By the time I am back in the car
the headless horseman
has gone home to his headless wife.

But as I walk, stars become tinny,
                blown leaves become frogs and crabs.

## Unlimited Travel

Through the wall I hear the piano
and in the dirty glass and frame
of the Japanese print, the leaves are shaking.
Knowledge is a dangerous thing,
and through the settee
I can feel the cat sleeping.

Custer should have felt like this
when he touched his wife on the cheek
as she hunched at the door, crying,
and he muttered bravely
"I'm off for my last stand, dearest."
Inside, a negro servant fell against a clavichord.

Upstairs I can hear somebody
fall out of the bath and talking.
Earlier it was empty except for him
crouching in the washbasin,
his silken locks wetter, his sword
waving
defiantly and arrows looking
as assured of historical certainty
as only arrows can.

## Folk Tales of the Border Counties

The sky is as flat as the roof of this hot car,
and a comet is due. These villages have names
like dead poachers and midshipmen, and their shops
are stocked to the cheeks with old paperbacks.

At the top, the normal pictures of intrusions;
holding babies, sandwiches, or smiling with maps of hills.

I stand blinking with my father at an eclipse;
he is unshaven and I feel a great sadness.

The strange men leaning on gates or dirty walls
have the same dogs every year, walking the wet bridges.

Eventually the comet blazes over trees in a dated fashion
and my mother pulls down the vanity mirror to check her face.
Sometimes the speeches of Sir Winston become too much for her,
and she has to turn to me at breakfast
to say something profound and husky.

## Exchange

From a telephone box on North Uist
I speak to the wrong mother. Lost
connections make these islands
more like fish, make ferryboats
into trawlers catching only last
week's newspapers and men with faces.

Lost connections
push you out of telephone boxes
with a bemused smile, your faith
in numbers shaken. "The
beach seemed like the best place to go."
Or home.

From a telephone box on North Uist
a lost connection can form the last
line of a witty postcard. It becomes
difficult to write home when you miss
connections with yourself, facing the lost
seas of mirror, empty boats crossing beaches.

# A Handbook of Suffolk Churches

## 1. IKEN

In R.H. Dove's book, *Church Bells in Britain*,
Iken is down as a four-bell tower. I had to walk
past a barking animal, through a field of stones,
to discover that the roof had gone, that they
were digging for Saxon evidence, that services
were held in ten feet near the table, boarded off.
Services were held monthly, tightly, by the ruff,
gripped to stop them blowing over the fields, held
to stop them rushing past the empty wall-space,
flying like ladies' scarves and hats, over into
the water near an old boat called Robin. Ropes
of the bells were tied high above a wheelbarrow
and they flapped in the wind which shuddered
even the Saxon evidence in pre-bag jugs below
the grass. As the ropes moved, twitching tails,

stray notes, blown from the Maltings, a mile away
across the water, soaked up into the bell-mouths
of the four bells, humming a little, to make sounds
which were carried away from me and the wild hound,
across marshland to a resort where they were no doubt
appalled by the general hubbub and noise of the tide.

## 2. SUFFOLK CHURCHES

All those churches we saw, gripping hills like flies,
sliding through fields like a straw church
carried in a ceremony, or leaning to catch
the whispered conversation of the dead, were like us,

running down the pebbles of the beach to the sea,
a beachcomber's paradise; shaken to the bag's bottom.

The ships, far out to sea, are floating churches
covered in barnacles, breasting huge waves, pews
rolling from aisle to aisle, or a stained glass
window, shattering
                    as inward the saint's face breaks

open. So having slid to the shirt-tail of the beach,
we watch a dozen gutted, filleted fish skeletons
being gathered up by the eccentric fish-doctor's hands.

He smiles. His broad lips form the base line
for the next in a series of thoughtful sunsets
which have slumped over the sky
                    like red dogs in front of the fire.


### 3. AT FELIXSTOWEFERRY

As though lemmings had actually found a bridge!

Our map was out of date, and where there should
have been a boat, lines of cars, old men in caps,

There was a family of cold people, throwing wood
into the calm; and ten houses impassively close.


There was also an old, torn ferry notice, with old
times, old information, old graffiti and alterations.

A pub shouts for help. Feeling white, we move home
over land, suddenly ancient, on the beaten charts.

As though brave Tommies had found no boats at Dunkirk!

## Ruined House, Saddleworth Moor

Stones are the outcome of years of thought;
studied walls are just door-hinges of body, or
dark paintings of the Plough dragging horses
with clouds over sky; froth on a grey stream
painted by a young man too near the moor's foreshore.

Shining on the floor, they are like the ages
of a room, stars which will be wet during a hot
summer; darkness, when it comes, stands
translating a relative, built for a departing train.


## In a Mist

"Hit him in the mouth! In the mouth!
He's a saxophone player!" Paul Whiteman,
King of Jazz, in his overweight days,
reflecting all the white tiles
of the spacious Whiteman Club toilets,
shouting orders to running waiters
for no reason at all in C.

The saxophonist, Paul Cartwright,
left his sax resting on the angular stand.
The waiters had a rundown of the First,
some say the best, World War,
around the jazzman's face, mostly
his lips. It was only a bit like
a solo. Teeth castanetting the urinal,
the long heave for breath.

Bix, grounded in the phalanx
of Goldkette's band, Whiteman's army,
played hard clouds, scapes, figures,
on his cornet, taking clarity at intervals

from a teacup of bright light, never
wincing like the younger people did.
He heard nothing of the sax player
being knocked into the crapper
although liquid makes the ear tender.

The waiters wiped the blood from their
smiles. Whiteman found a baton from some
where in his jacket, left the tiles, left
Vic Berton, Master of the Hot Tympani,
who had come to aid Cartwright, talking to
his friend on the floor, like wives
and husbands in a hard bed. As Bix played
the waiters carried teacups back and here
to the bandstand. Bix hardly ever collapsed.


## Slug Death

Tuesday

At Gringley-on-the-hill, North Notts, Mr. King
struggles with a bell. A vicar and two visitors
glance, and a child pulls hands in a crib with
straw and figurines. My talent has dribbled
over into bright catalogues of ways to saunter
down a corridor; my book is a marriage to one
planet, mostly water, and I must remain faithful.

Saturday

All-night movies in the badlands of the soul.
Reel one: In the Basement Sales Area, after
stairs, and Hazel said "Nobody paints the sea
as it should be painted." Reel two: Walking
with Tag through Doncaster, meeting his father.
Tag is wordless; he bubbles, jibs, spits, says
"We're going to the cinema", and the crowds.
Attacking trees and a wife laughing easily.

(Between the cushions and frames of plays,
my response is, quite unexpectedly, Easy Chair:
Easy Chairing my outlook, Easy Chair historical
inevitability, Easy Chair in alone-face and
three-piece-suite alignment. My toast, like me,
is singed under the grill; I was crisp in Phoenix
at two o'clock in the morning, watching aroad,
or during that other crackling San Antonio night.

Sunday

Golly, after all this, I am on a corner,
a road which I have travelled by double-decker
and never walked. Today I am in a car
sailing to Bentley, South Yorkshire, five bells,
tenor five hundredweights with other persons to
ring although the church is not well congregated
and the evening service is sung in the vicar's
lounge. Jane Wood is not used to the inside work
of bob doubles, and Mr. King shouts at her head.

The bells are so light and you must ring them
carefully. A row of handbells is hung to a "wall".
You must go gingerly on the bell at Bentley
with a girl. Deep mutual human need and shirts.


## The Sea Slides Down to the Land's Edge

This village has been fired from a ship's cannon
and the range was wrong. The houses
are clinging to the cliffs like plants.

In here, with waiters and a small girl,
we are seeing films of famous lecturers:
Frankenstein informs us of very little
unless it is a message about being more careful

16

with other peoples' brains and bodies.
Dracula speaks about trances being difficult to escape;
he says that madmen will always babble and roll their eyes
until someone believes them and smiles indulgently.

This tower has been dropped from a zeppelin
to frighten the people. Over the years
it has almost, though not quite, taken root.


## Madmen on Ferries

Between island and island these boys laugh,
shocking the funnels, making me turn to my crisps.
Above the sound of a child counting seagulls,
a portly chap from Lincoln talks loudly
while downstairs lads in caps wrestle with sheep.

One, near Islay, shouting MORNING
all afternoon; his brother perhaps
lurching amongst cases as we leave South Uist.
His suit is the most insane thing about him,
and Strange Philippa runs up and down the jetty
looking for her lost fisherman,
while I point out a seal to no one listening
which disappears as soon as my eyes are turned.


## The Long Silences

These silences are longer than a piece of string,
like an old proverb whose words have been stretched to death.
Speaking to you is like stepping over a moth on the stairs,
and the long silences move across the room like fog.

17

You are opposite me, even when you sit beside my face.

The Consul's Wife, in *Under the Volcano*
lifts her eyes to the ceiling and sees him through a bottle
as men trapped in a submarine are watched by a frond of seaweed,
or balloonists are unnoticed by steeplejacks who drop their
    sandwiches
and look down to a man pointing up and shouting.

The long silences ought to be broken
by the discovery of a print in the sand
or even, in an empty bus shelter, a dry sentence.

Touching you is a strange kind of punctuation
with hard full stops between sentences as sticky as dry paint.
This empty Hebridean island receives daily bags of silence
even though a map-maker spoke its name once, to a secretary.

The Consul's Wife in *Under the Volcano* finds a dying man by the
    roadside.
He is groaning at the dirt; she whispers to a restive horse,
as newscasters speak to couples kissing on settees,
or steeplejacks are ignored by balloonists playing cards and
    reading.


## Call Me Irresponsible

A small toy Lego church
dropped from the back of a gig

into this field to please the locals
by the Man as he passed through to the big house

no ladder in this church to reach any bells
only names, the same names, over the walls

18

pit owners, dead as snow
adored by the broken electric fire and the old pews

the dead mouse on the step distils so much
forces it all into a small Kodachrome

of me and him with pints
on a hill above the dark cricket field

and the pub overflowing with suburbia
and rugby shirts tucked into something

ignoring the stable which ignores itself
and the blacksmith's building festooned with remoulds

reflected light as I gaze up
glinting in the eye of the giant dead mouse

which crashes into my glass and body
after falling for so long from a field cracked like a egg.


## They Were Not Ordinary Bandits

Place with the most pain
is the place;
this must be the place.

The moon never shines
on a dark night.

Time with the most pain.

This time. Now we move.
Here is the prodigal moon.
I slaughter the fatted

house of my sleep.
Here are the gifts:
the harsh lights,
the staring eyes.

Sleep with the most pain
is the three o'clock meeting.
I clap my knuckles
on the empty sheepfold
of your sleeplessness.
Depth, depth.

Hold the chip shop counter
as though it was cold.
Look into the eyes
of the chip shop lady
as though they were solid.
Wake up. Soon
we will be walking home,
singing on the way to home.

Singing will mean: Awake.
Home will mean: Night.

We are awake until we reach
the night; none of us
survives until we die.
Where is the gift of depth?


## Barge Journey

Now I can accept the old Yorkshire legend
about the man who strolled through a rhubarb-forcing shed
and came out wearing a green hat.

We are a mile from anywhere except here
and the trick is to convince yourself
that you are not riding on the heads of the trees
which stand upside-down to attention
in this skin-still model of the water.

Now I can accept the old Yorkshire legend
about the man who put his head in a horsetrough
and came up with his hair full of horses.

I am a yard from anyone except myself;
if I do a quick impersonation of a barge
perhaps the water will gather around me,
petrol will be poured into my ears
and I will have no memory of a time before canals.

Now I have become the old Yorkshire legend
about the man who got on a barge
and was later left in the water,
while the barge walked through the streets
to a house full of men, women and barges.


## Treatise

Scrooge's remarkable spiritual turnabout in the last chapter,
compared to that man in overalls
hesitating at the door because he sees the steam
and the boy waving his arms
(scalding) (making tea)
makes sense when looked at in the light of
the chipshop in Nairn with the tiny man
and the tracts and pamphlets all over the counter
next to the pop and peanuts, near the harbour.

## The Crazy Horse Interview

The time is riper than it should be;
a day has gone brown, and the sky
is looking daggers at a town without hats.
Across the building site
Arthur crackles an anecdote
through the tin cans and stretched wire
of our shared experience of the gale
which is tipping the bricks from Ted's hod.

Crazy Horse, the hyper-active man who shouts
all the time, is running towards us. Sometimes
he is called Cracker Jack. Sometimes his nicknames
are misheard or misquoted; to some people
he is War Horse; to Stan he is Laughing Jack.
So to the whole site he is a wild man
with a thousand names, like the wind
is a mad horse with a thousand names.

The weekend starts here
with a new wind-myth
which cracks its way into our heads
rendering the rest useless.
Like the best myths
it blinds and deafens us,
like the best myths
it will blind and deafen itself.

## Fame

News on the radio of fires
reminds me of the Bowley family.
The daughter June ate sandstone.
I was ushered upstairs once to see

22

her mother Emma with the new baby.
On the night before they went over
the sea to a new life in Australia
their old van caught fire, and the dad
who was a strange man with a lot of gypsy
ran repeatedly with a washing-up bowl,
splashing it over the engine, as
Uncle Charlie and my Auntie watched
from a next door window. Australia
was the place to go in the Sixties.
Keith Barlow, who built rockets, went
to Australia with his toy soldiers.
Annette who kissed at parties
went to Australia with her awful brother.
Some of my friends went further than that.
The problem is that the living ones
can represent eternity much better than the dead.
I can still see the curve where Dave ended,
but June Bowley will always be chewing rocks
beneath an exploding sun in a flat desert
landscape
photograph.

*Dave Godfrey 1956-1973*


## No Still Point

The awful middle area; groping
for common ground without hope
(or with hope, it makes no odds).
In the dark, on the bus, between
kisses; the need for contact.

Day clicks around the night's
revolving door. Some bastard
has invented the joke, smug

in its belief that the world
is somehow capable of reduction.

I remember stumbling once
into a new year down a hill;
it was raining; I was soaked.
A terminal drunk was slumped
over the bridge-rails above
the disused canal. He wore
the suit, the special suit
for drunks, crumpled and sad.

The awful middle area. Speech
should be prefaced by a scream
and punctuated with a series
of hostile gestures. It would be

easier. The suit moved, groaned,
spoke to me as I walked home
into next year. By the sports field
light began to break, the rain
began to change colour.

## On the Impossibility of Staying Alive

They have found a new moon;
it stands on my shoulder.
They call it moon because
they lack imagination.
I call it moon because
I lack all conviction.

It has another name,
but that name, like God's
is terrible to pronounce.
It is terrible to pronounce

like Czrcbrno, a hamlet
in the Balkans. The moon
calls itself moon because
it lacks self-knowledge.

This moon sometimes whispers
and you never heard such rubbish.
I listen because I lack strength,
I smile because I have no muscles
with which to frown. At certain times
of the day, the moon hides.

When I am an old man
with flour in my beard, and
packs of incontinence pants
on the sideboard, the moon
will still be new, and will be
perpetually discovered as new
by generations of scientists.
The moon is not a nice man.

## The Story So Far

FRANK, an eccentric surrealist millionaire,
is in mourning for his surrealist wife WENDY
who has just died. JESUS, an eccentric

surrealist millionaire, has brought her back
from the dead, but has not told FRANK.
FRANK, meanwhile, has sold all his eccentric

surrealist companies and has rented a cockle
boat in COLWYN BAY. He meets WANDA, the daughter
of WILL SHAKESPEARE, a surrealist eccentric.

SURREALIST, the cockle boat, sinks in the
purple and red bay during a surrealist
storm of table-legs and 'cellos. Eccentric

surrealist FRANK discovers his wife WENDY
walking about at the bottom of the sea
in a diving suit. JESUS, in an eccentric

surrealist fashion, has put her there.
FRANK is amazed to find WENDY still
alive; but what will he tell WANDA?

Now read on.


## Responses to Industrialisation

The roads to Hell were paved;
that much we could deduce.
The rest was guesswork.

Door-frames were always the hope of the world, always
ajar or closed, sometimes open,
but never "seen-to-be-burning"
until now.

Was it not curious that
whichever side of the doorway you stood
you could always see the interior of the cottage?

Yes, it was (mighty) curious.

Purity of diction is one thing, but

it brings us to now, to the time
when I am toasting my Collected Essays
before a sometimes flickering,
sometimes roaring, grandchild.


## With Chris at the Barriers

We're in the queue with the poems.
"How long have you been on it?"
I ask, fingering his five lines
about a cat, and his twelve lines
about the pit. The slow coal train
humps over small faults on the rail,
each carriage lifting like a boy
to a blessing, or a dog to a blow.

The red lights flick as he answers.
"Two years; but I was on the sick
a year when I lost my eye." Trucks
move along the lines like cats over lumps
in the rug. He has two eyes to my mind;
they are red, and narrow. The train limps
to a halt behind the barriers telling
us to stay. "The sight in my eye, I mean."

Of course, Chris. I'm sorry. The barriers
lift, the red lights go out, glowing,
and the two lines of traffic cross
each other over the railway like friends
on a street in a war they have lost.

## Tankersley Tunnel

1.  Imagine a parrot
    between a train
    and a track.

2.  Now the mouth slaps the driver
    across the face

    and in the black I
    am inside and out the window.

    Paradoxical bastard.

    Now the dark licks the driver
    along the back
    and the clumsy moon fumbles
    for a door in the clouds.

3.  Now forget the parrot.

4.  I said: forget the parrot.

## Apple-Blossom Time

My slim anthology of Third World War Poets
slipped from the shelf at ten past six,

and the 6.09 Pullman train was exactly
a minute late. I ran to my window;

across the fields a stiff breeze ruffled
a herd of cows. Two lovers glanced

upwards from a gate. The sky was the colour
of the sky, but there was a stench.

"Take care, but remember
to bring it back intact!"

I shouted. They laughed, and I froze
in a useless position

like the dog on the cover
of the jumble sale Girls Own Annual.


## Melville's "Treasure Island"

Young Hawkins tells me that the ship is bottomless,
but I haven't been below to check.
We sent a man to the crow's nest a week ago,
and he hasn't been back.

This feels like a big ship.

We seem to be stuck
to the harbour walls.
I don't think we're even floating.

Maybe we are becalmed (this
is my first voyage); how
can we find Captain Kidd's gold
if we do not move?

Blind Pugh stands on the bridge
holding an ear-trumpet,
listening for treasure.

This is my first voyage
but I thought that, on a ship,
there was at least the *sensation*
of movement.

I may be wrong.

Tomorrow
he opens the map.

## Life on Earth

When he came in
she gave him a flower
called "Welcome Home Husband
However Drunk You Be".

I am not drunk, he said;
this is not my home,
I am not your husband.

"Three mistakes
do not change the name of a flower"
she replied.

## How the Hornpipe Failed

Generous scene-setter.

It is, undoubtedly, a trick
of the abstract imagination;
you seem to be a boy who
has not lived with objects;

How, how
do you pull the invisible rope
through your thin hands?

Scene-setter, area
behind the trees,
never lived with objects
only with the music which

was not produced. And now
you ask me how to love.

Is not the invisible rope
in your hands enough,
scene-dancer?


## Form without Implicit Moral

It is almost nine o'clock. The women
are taking the children down to school.
They pass a man who is trembling
controllably
with a big machine. As they walk
white smoke
begins to climb from a chimney,
and the sun holds itself out
from behind a cloud onto Keppel's
Column,
tall on a rise behind the half-built streets.
The only word I can think of
to describe the scene
is "outfit",
and that is the wrong word,
is completely the wrong word.

# "Ilkley Moor Baht 'at": Amplification

Chill against his hair, and the wind
pushing itself through the long roots
of treeless waste. He almost sneezes
in the tight trembling cold, turns up
his collar and tugs his cap down over

two memories which are more real,
though slightly less tangible,
than the paper he holds in his pocket.

First memory, a morning like this.
The cold turf opening cold as a fridge door,
the six of them lowering the body
into the shallow hole. A few
words about the weather, no hymns,
brief movements with gardening tools.

Second memory, an evening in town.
The six of them around a long table
as full of ducks as ten ponds;
eating, holding brittle Northern talk
on a wet evening under the hills
exactly ten years after a friend's death.

And the piece of paper. A loose sonnet
in the dead man's typing: "To Mary Jane",
and underneath in her best neat writing
an agreement to meet on the moors.

Chill against his hair, the song
of a duck reaches him from the high
branches of treeless waste. He
crushes the paper. The foolish living
will always eat the stupid dead
without knowing it. His cap blows off
in the cold wind of a duck's wings.

## Pithead Workings, Darfield

The dilemma of the ribbed sunrise
through the misted window of his breath
underlines the topographical lie.

The truth must be dragged out
like rusty metal from a pond;

the perfect curves
dripping water to water
from a moon
to a shifting bicycle light
stealing inches from death.

## The Female Drummer

To think I was a drummer
and a maiden all the while.

I hung myself beneath a horse
and scraped my uncovered head
along the road's noise.

To think of the narrow topcoat
of a failing religion
and a maiden all the while.

To think of the deflating lungs
of a crushed belief
and a maiden all the while.

You may call it confusion;
I swing beneath a horse.

In a secondary, tertiary
landscape like this
there is little, else.

To think I was a drummer
with my fine cap and feathers.

In a dream I stuck myself
to the bottom of a boat.

The tide beat retreat.
Such skin is a dream

and a maiden.

*Darfield Main Colliery, July 1981*

## *Isolated Row of Houses near the Pit*

Nothing stands in the way of me.

Slope your minds gently
that I may climb them without effort.

Comedy may not be
the correct response

now that the world has the mind
of its own and not its own mind.

My eyes are continually red.
Issue this warning: those
who live by the sword shall die

in their own time.

# Elegy for an Hour of Daylight

The tilt of the Earth is beautiful;
the day is a yellow blanket and the twilight
is a ladybird on a yellow blanket.

Cramped, untoasted, the sky
will prove too tight for the sun.

Frank is flying to Dar-es-Salaam.
Phil is having a fight with his father
and is giving up the farm, again.

Cramped, lightly toasted, the sky
proves too tight for the sun,
bursts into a row of lamps

as the ladybird flies over
the yellow blanket. Phil
moves along the gouged lane
shouting with his father,

looking at a hen. The hen
leans over a puddle
and tilts her shadow
across the water.

From his aeroplane Frank sees
the shadow of his wing
pass over the hen's feathers,

sees the hung clouds
too tight for the sun
as though the air has been pressed

flat with a hot iron but
badly, leaving the ladybird's creases.

# Pigeon Men and a High Ladder

### 1.

In the marshy land at the back of the pigeon sheds
an enormous ladder has raised itself overnight.
They say many things about high ladders
in the George on a Friday night as they adjust
their pigeon clocks. It throws a shadow
across the tarmac of the yard to the Catholic School

and I climb it.
Not the ladder
but the shadow.

### 2.

The pigeon men flock out of the George door
and stand around me as I crawl.
At the top of the ladder
my hollow head brushes something.
"What has tha found, lad?"
They ask. A wall.
I have found a wall.

### 3.

I asked him, I said, what
has tha found, lad, what?
Then he painted a small
thing on my door. I said
what's that, lad, what's that?

What has tha painted on my door?
What is it, lad, what?

# Simultaneous Evening and Morning
### Norfolk, May 1982

Bathers are moving to the water
and from the water in the same

long step of the waves over sand,
the same step of shoes over sand.

The sun has been hung from a tree
until dead.

Remember the sunset's
bitter taste of blood
in the Moon's mouth
as the headlights
became uncertain
along the beach-road.

An owl looks at the watch
on a cock's wrist; they've

been fighting again
for possession of the space
above the skylark;

the six p.m. train
tapped on the tent door
and pokes morning's torch
into their eyes,
                    true check
                    local papers.

# Poem Badly Translated from the Language

Tell me why you have died and when
in not more than ten words.

How many pains can dance
on the head of an angel?

How many angels can dance
on the head of a man?

How tedious your nightmares are.
How commonplace your visions.

The future is a hailstone with a fish in it.
The past is a fish beside a broken hailstone.

The Blues is the ancient Chinese art
of folding paper until it cries.

The coffee-bar mode is not enough;
1959 is an aspect of a face
viewed from a subway. The far
mask of the Moon is always turned
from us but we are aware of the smell.

Revive the old native insult:
point at me with one of your eyes
and I shall slip into the tight neck of Hell.

Note: Little is known of the author of this poem. His only other known
work is a single line, barely translatable, which could be rendered as
"Songs, built like temporary shelters, contain music and words."

# Broadened by Travel

He marches, with a long column of men,
by a Post Office in Northern China.
It is 1945. He says to himself
"I will have many sons.
There will be no more wars."

Father. Here I am. I am three
of your sons and I am in a tree.

The summer will slip into December
as it always did. Christmas Day
picnics in the bright blue, under
the tree. I am unborn on a branch
looking at your head's thoughts.

A tree is growing through
floor after floor
of a Post Office in Northern China.
The roof is approaching.
There will be no more floors.


# The Harsh Stink of Mythical
# European Gypsy Violins

Fiddler play at my table,
I will retreat from the light
which is what we call a route

still in the planning stage,
the rare birds, rare orchids
people in cardboard farmhouses

safe against this particular wind.
I remember the embroidery troupe
coming to our village every year

presenting of course a history
of the long world in samplers,
teacloths, cushion covers,

here and there a face was noted
to be my own or your own,
we bought up the stock,

fired it, buried it
twice in the same box
because of a long lifetime

and soil erosion, inertia
marsh-diseases, freeze.


## The Sum of the Parts

The tall Irishman leans across the table
to tell me that his eyes are everywhere.
He is seeking, I am told, a divorce.
He tells me he prefers to know
exactly who is his enemy. *I had*
*plain clothes, and still I was recognised.*

Gypsies make him uncertain. *Their caravans,*
*I'm telling you their caravans are immaculate, inside.*

He can't sleep. *Ah, I can't stand the nights!*

His massive hands fashion a transparent knitted article
in the air, level with his pulsing neck.
He climbed, once or twice. *Dartmoor, Bodmin Moor,
these things called tors.*

He had plain clothes, and still
*he was recognised.*


## The Old Agony of the Scalp

There is a crisis in modern cricket,
no new players are coming from the counties
and I am a spiritual Mexican
dancing on my hat until I sink
into the main street.

It is the old agony of the scalp,
amigos. The schools play almost
exclusively football, rugby;
ah the children they would choose

rockabilly if they could. A true
crisis, exacerbated by the hot power
of the English sun, the macho
mentality which says

"Tomorrow, tomorrow
I will organise the raffle to buy
the stumps, pads, umpires."

The English Disease: The Wasting in Heat.
"Dick Turpin's in his greenhouse,
his cottage is covered in ivy"
as my great-grandfather used to say,
offering the joke and explaining the joke.

41

The old agony of the performing seal, greatly
missed old man. I still see you breathing
heavily in the stupid altitude of the
cricket pavilion in the high mountains,
mourning the lack of players from the villages.


## Lamentation

There is a constant humming in the scripture room.
Lol Chappell is reading to us from Amos
and there is a constant humming noise.

A boy called Smithies once hid in a cupboard
and leaped out at Lol Chappell in the scripture room.
The constant humming noise is a prank.

There is a track near the school called Golden Smithies lane
which the boys pass when they run cross-country.
Smithies is nothing like a god.

Lol Chappell lives in Canada now and he fishes on a lake.
He dozes in a canoe and he wears a big hat.
He barks and the humming stops;

across the still water of the lake
the silence is the silence
of a boy about to burst from a cupboard.

## Own Goal: Waiting on the Pier

I wait on the small island with a few others
for the boat bringing the parcels,
for the boat bringing the last episode
of *The Old Curiosity Shop*. The boat
moves enigmatically through the thin weather.

I study the well-muscled back of the girl
ahead of me in the queue. For weeks
we have waited together like this, as Little Nell
moves slowly to the centre of her desert city.

Quilp, last month, held her under
in a bucket of icy water, and she sang psalms
and recited her letters. I saw the girl
weeping as she read by the reliable light
of the lighthouse which also gives time

to digest the words
as it pulls its light away across the fields
leaving us in the darkness with our magazines.
The girl is a dancer. As the boat approaches
she dances a dance called

"In The Brown Room of the Evening,
Little Nell, Little Nell,
I Pretend You Are A Lighthouse
Lighting our Lives Once A Month;
I Pretend That I Have Known You
and Your Gentle Grandfather."

The people on the pier stare at her. Some begin to weep,
some experience terror, some giggle, some forget.

I turn from the water and crawl toward the forest,
singing my letters, reciting psalms.

# The "Owl Brand" Range of Embarrassment Lotions

A full shelf.

Little Owl Cream
for hot climes.

Barn Owl Cream
for the countryside
after dark.

The ship pitched.

Nelson's Owl Cream
(he smiled)
for embarrassment
in an otherwise
heroic situation.

The ship shuddered.

All the jars
almost empty.

Long Eared Owl Cream
for those moments at sea.

He hesitated.

The insistent knocking at the door.

Tawny Owl Cream,
Thrust Owl Cream,

a shelf as long as the cabin.

He took down all the jars,
smeared all the cream
over and over.

He opened the door.

The man in the rigging
aimed

at the easy, shining, target.


## Loose

*'I offered myself a tent; but I did not accept it'* (Arab proverb)

Men are not seahorses. I am not
a seahorse. I am many things but
I am not in any way a seahorse.

Please accept that I am serious.

I am not in any way a seahorse.
Seahorses have no meaning for me.
I have never seen a seahorse
and seahorses may not exist.

There is to be no joke ending.
This is no O. Henry seahorse denial.
No twists in the tail.
Surrealism also is abhorrent to me.

If I continue to speak about seahorses
I will cry bitterly,
dabbing my eyes with a seahorse.

## The Red Indian Rugby Team "Strange Names XV" Land on a Lonely Irish Beach

Wingless Crow never really wanted to come. He wrings
out his soaking shorts, uneasy about his nakedness.
"Gods still exist in Ireland" says Unhappy Tree.

A crab moves across the beach. "Here
is an Irish God" the players shout.
"God of the Great Scrum" says Unhappy Tree.

The pack pack into a scrum and head towards
the crab. "I want to meet a God"
mutters High Water from the second row.

At sunset they huddle by a small fire
eating hot crab. "Edible Gods, invisible men,
surely this is Paradise!" cries Grass-Puller.

Darkness covered the whole beach as they
practised a line-out, using
an imaginary ball. The ball
was their unseen God,
hastily adopted.


## A Room Opposite Hilton's Drapery, Brough

The lightning is a momentary heron
with no head and a body hidden
by clouds; the thunder drowns, from
inside, the voices of the persons
whose car "broke down up the road":

"We'll have a strip-wash,
We'll have a strip-wash."

The drainpipe down Hilton's
is a line of saliva to the street;
the momentary heron's taut
leg plants a foot behind the hills.

The sauntering storm strip-washes
the broken-down walls, the heron
dips his toes into our head
and breaks up down the road
as the sun burgles the heron's nest
like a bright fish slipping from the sea
after and before a brace of freak waves.

And in the trough between the waves
there is the sound of tap-water:
Life reflecting speech, reflecting storm.


## Tetchy Improvisation on Early Eighteenth-Century Film Criticism

*'This new medium is merely an excuse for Death'*
(Anonymous film critic, 1726)

The death of the excuse!
It's all an excuse for Death, all this talking;
If the sloppy King of Kings
hadn't felt the rain on his head
then there wouldn't be the need
for all this talking.

I blame the slovenly King of Kings, myself.
These damned silly sunsets!
Damn' red wig slipping, if you ask me;

the scruffy King of the World
burping and hiccuping
on the World's knee.

All an excuse for Death!
Usherette like a moon in November,
seats like a forest of seats.
A feeble excuse, too. I prefer Death.

On this shore, here, f'r instance: waves
pounding out a point like a wet-nurse slapping
a dying King-baby with a breast. (Storm!)

It's all, in all, an excuse.
I came in out of the rain.
I sat in the dark and blinked.
It's all, all in all, an excuse.

You know how I mean. This
this darkness this music
and this movement this
this excuse. For Death.

Death, the only coach!
On the only road!

Until now.


## The Soft White Pillowcase Boys

Five poets and a children's novelist
resident in a college garden
on a long September afternoon.

Two bottle-green corduroy suits,
one dress, one brown suit, one
jacket and casual trousers.

One jeans and sweatshirt
sweaty from the Edinburgh Fest,
clutching his Scotsman reviews.

We are The Soft White Pillowcase Boys.
Our tribal name was adopted this morning
during the coffee and sherry session.

The jacket and casual trousers
had looked over his sweet black cup
directly at the Head of Department.

"Coming up the motorway, the fog..."
The Head of Department smiled.
"...was like a soft white pillowcase..."

He had used the line earlier
on the typist at her desk as we waited
to begin the session.

He had honed it since. The true
art of the poet, the craftsman
at his ink-stained bench.

## Pushed Home when the Clouds were still Raw

Pushed home when the clouds were still raw,
tallying the shifts in the day's emphasis,
from Regular Nights leaning across a sink
to Regular Days pointing out over a table.

The first light, like skin from a knuckle,
hurts despite itself; the second light
bends the head over a book, increasing
its knowledge, but also increasing

its size.

We speak of little else, your honour.
as the day soaks the clothes of the unwary
like a tidal bore.

Plants have to be re-potted, calendars turned,
paperweights breathed on, domestic interiors
plumped or shaken.

## From the Section Dealing with the Loss of Grace

And the priest shall answer:
*Walk past the white caravans*

The communicant shall walk past the white caravans.
At the fifth caravan, the greyhound
shall burst from the darkness
and shall bite both legs of the communicant.
The faces shall appear at the caravan windows.

And the gypsy women shall shout:
*Kick it, mister. Kick it, mister.*

Alternative Forms:

A: The communicant shall kick the dog.
B: The communicant shall not kick the dog,
    and shall continue to walk past the white caravans.

If alternative B is followed
the priest shall say the following:
*Enough. Shout back the greyhound.*
*Switch off the bedroom light which is always on.*

The dog shall be called back, the communicant
shall pass the house where the bedroom light
is always on, and the light shall go out.
A passing grit-wagon shall spray the communicant.

It is imperative that at the moment when the communicant
is sprayed, an empty bus shall pass the communicant
in the other direction. The communicant shall remain silent.


## The Tennis Ball Factory Poems

### 1.

Everywhere the lines; the balls.
Long, long fluorescent lights.
By the coffee machine, the restless
attempts for change in purses.
The enormous laughing woman, there.
and the man studying the back pages.
Everywhere the lines. The balls
falling in lines from the broken
conveyor, landing on the greased
head of a man in a white coat.
Early in the evening at the bottom
of the gently sloping ramp a boy
tackles me about crossword puzzles.
Everywhere the lines, the balls.

2.

The manager who is about to go insane
holds up to me in the early hours
of a hot morning in Summer

a piece of rubber and a massive spider.
"Still alive," he says: "still alive Mac."

Later in the canteen I tell George.
He mishears me: "Aye, Mac, we're just
grovelling in the bastard dust, just
crawling in the bastard muck."

And somewhere, just, the spider
is still alive in the night sky.


3.

The accumulated straightness of it all.
Huge steel straightness within which
Charlie sells chocolate, pens, birthday cards.

Why are the wicked so strong?

Not you, Charlie, not you.
Sell me your goods.


4.

A dog peeps into the noisy room.
The manager who will go insane
puts on his "dog-in-the-factory" face
and throws a meaningless name
into the bouncing air.

Later he will forget this, later
I remember his face
as he spoke to the dog's indifference.

5.

The two women are fighting
near the office. Some workers
notice, some see nothing.

Until one of them is locked
in the office and the other
runs home, they are fighting.

A future composed simply
of the present. Men running
against angular, clicking

machines to a fight.


6.

Talk to me without moving your
lips; without inviting any doors
to pop open, sell me your

unfortunate tendency to
speak, speak or to fall
silent. Upstairs, I dress.

"You call this a life?"
shouts Albert the Fitter
looking down at my hair

from his enormous height,
and I say something small,
negative, about seeing,

waiting. Albert and the back
of his long RAF neck
lean into the machine.

applying grease. Upstairs
I take positive steps.

7.

The telephone rings at five o'clock in the morning.
No one in the canteen
moves. We have lost our bastard hands.

## Frosted

It is night with the speed
of water becoming coffee
and the snow has almost gone;
only a heap is left, off-white,
shovelled, by the garage.
They have opened the wine
to let it breathe.

Hold up your thumb.
Do not let the pulse
interfere.

It is morning with the speed
of a cup emptying. Dregs
go out, flung over the yard
towards the garage, black
and brown on the half-dark snow.
The air is breathing hard,
staining the sky wider.

If you put your hand here
some days or here
on other days you can feel
the baby kicking me.

Hold up your thumb.
Do not let the pulse
interfere.


## The Meaning of Life
### (A Yorkshire Dialect Rhapsody)

From under't canal like a watter-filled cellar
coming up like a pitman from a double'un, twice,
I said "Hey, you're looking poorly"
He said "Them nights are drawing in"

Down't stairs like a gob-machine, sucking toffees,
up a ladder like a ferret up a ladder in a fog,
I said "Hey, you're looking poorly"
He said "Half-a-dozen eggs"

Over't top in't double-decker groaning like a whippet
like a lamplighter's daughter in a barrel full of milk,
I said "Hey, you're looking poorly"
He said "Night's a dozen eggs"

Down't canal like a barrow full of Gillis's parsnips,
coming up like a cage of men in lit-up shiny hats,
I said "Hey, you're looking poorly"
He said "Half a dozen nights"

Under't canal on a pushbike glowing like an eggshell
up a ladder wi' a pigeon and a brokken neck,
I said "Hey, you're looking poorly"
He said "I feel like half-a-dozen eggs"

Over't night on a shiny bike wi' a lit-up hat,
perfect for't poorly wi' heads like eggs,
I said "Hey, you died last week"
He said "Aye, did you miss me?"

## SF Novel

He slept past his stop,
lolling on the seat.

When we searched his face
all we found was a lip

cracked in the long heat.
We all spat at once.

We searched his face again
beside the high overpass

for the first whisper
of a splintered screen,

for the Heart of Carparkness,
caught in sudden rain.


## What Really Happened to the Buffalo

An hour before a poetry reading in Telford
and I'm as nervous as I always am.

I walk the pavement outside the pub
and the Iron Bridge holds itself
like a picture in a frame. Inside, Ian McMillan
is nervous. I walk the pub yard.

The power of the text is endless;
endless to reply to itself, endless
to refer to itself,

like a cheque referred to a drawer.
Ian McMillan trembles in the pub,
his poems quake in their little books

and, outside, I walk the pub yard,
his American-Indian-With-The-Secret.

The power of the text heats me, lights me,
sheens my feathers, polishes my buckskin,
Brother can you spare? Wait here;
Ian McMillan is pacing the toilets.
Brother,
I know what happened to the buffalo:

I know why the plains once full
are now as empty as they now are.

Ian McMillan the audience
is waiting. No, brother, wait,
tonight I am your buffalo.

I will whisper,
brother, what really happened
to the buffalo. The audience,
Ian McBuffalo. Ian McWidePlain-
with-no-buffalo; the audience.

Iron bridge, you are like a space
in the space where the buffaloes were.

The audience, brother, spare, buffalo, endless to refer.

## For me

For me,
if it's not got rockers
it's not a chair.
It's just a pile of sticks,
and you can pick a pile of sticks up
on the street.

For me,
if there's no flaps on the pockets
it's not a suit.
It's just a piece of cloth,
and you can pick a piece of cloth up
on the street.

For me,
if you can't lock it
it's not a briefcase.
It's just a bit of leather,
and you can pick a bit of leather up
on the street.

So here's me,
rocking backwards and forwards on my chair,
flapping the flaps on my suit,
locking and unlocking my briefcase,
and trying to sick a splat of rhyme
on my verse to make it complete.

And you can't fault that:
it's neat.

## Peace: Be Still

The point of your story
is that anecdote is dead.

It died reaching for something

that pointed in the grass
like an arrow to the trees:

the trees that meant so much
in the story, but nothing
in the poem. Peel the sticky tape
away from the doll's mouth.

Long live
the way we look tonight;

at the choking entrance
to Queens Midtown Tunnel
a boy on a skateboard
zips between the cars
offering orange juice

and behind him the sun
is the colour of shapeless.


## Why are you Ringing

Why are you ringing, now?
I asked you not to contact me;
every detail is finalised.

I managed to get the dogs,
all of them. The house stinks
and the neighbour has begun

to bark back. It is too late
to change the plan. I
built the box like you said,

and painted it the right colour;
I tied the basket to the balloon,
and I placed the telescope

in the correct window. There
is no point in you ringing me;
it would be too late to change

even if we wanted to change.
The eagle and the boy have
already gone through the post;

barring the possibility of storms
they will be there tomorrow night.
All is in hand. But I tell you

this. This is my last job.
I am sick to here with it.
I can no longer speak

without laughing, I can no
longer skip down the street
without howling. I have had

enough. Remember the code-
words: "Everyone puts out
more than they take in"

I must go: the man is here
with the multicoloured water.
We are on schedule,

please don't ring again.

# Two Miners Pass
## in Opposite Directions at Daybreak

Four a.m. and the first cars
are going nowhere by the dark window.

Extra. Late Final. Read
nothing about it.
Read *noting* for *nothing*
later in the broke text.
I am noting everything you say.

Four fifty and the first light
is going by the window.

If the land had legs
they would be broken legs.
A bulb fills itself
by the dark wardrobe

mirror. A bus passes
with a huge noise of water.
Read noting about it.

The language strained,
sprains, snapped, broke.
The men spoke. Did not speak.

Five to five. Extra
sky has been drafted in.
Read all about it. I read
all about it yesterday.

Five o'clock and the sky
reads all about itself
in the wet road. Extra,

the words curled in the pockets
of the pit clothes. If the land
had legs they would be running
running.

I read all about it, yesterday.
I am nothing everything you say.

Every fine thing
you say.


## The Texas Swing Boys' Dadaist Manifesto

("I just want to hear/some Dadaist country songs"
Tex Schwitters, Abilene, March 1924)

black horse hat six
        gun    two fifty stranger

ON THUNDERING STAGECOACH WHEELS OF DADA!

take the brothers: grant meadows
                        chester meadows

two fifty stranger
still hands

HOT DURN! CRASHING SIXSHOT PISTOL SHOTS OF DADA!

it's high two fifty    on the broken clock
the menu                don't change

TEA, HONEY! GREAT CREAKING TABLE TOPS OF DADA!

nothing changes            and the clock            don't

TAKE A HANGING ROPE TO YOUR DOBRO POETICS

DOBRODADA!

hands up, clock

HONEY, THE DADA SUNSET WILL WALK INTO US!

("Rupert Brooke was/the greatest Dadaist of us all"
from Collected Letters of Zane Gray, Knopf, 1982)

*Recorded by The Texas Swing Boys, July 1924, at The Gospel
Studios, Austin*

## *Resident*

"There's a bloke there reading a book"
"I don't give a shit"

The view from the study window
never changes.

There is always the pit, always the scaffolding yard,
always a wagon loaded with battens.

Usually the rain. Usually
my family, her family,
spreading back across the yard,
usually Harry, dead six months,
Pete, walking his dog, Garry and Val,
and Darryl, and Harry, usually,
dead six months, and Pete,

and they say "Do you have time to write?"

I am writing this, on a train going through Irlam.

Every house on a certain street
for sale.
A white pony in a field of gorse.

On Piccadilly Station,
walking with her son,
between platform four and platform five

Is a woman with a well-trimmed beard.

Do you have time to write?
I am writing this.

"He's writing in the book now."
"I still don't give a shit."

## The Monster's Last Letters to his Children

> *"The bolty and the stitchy bloke*
> *is sitting at his desk..."*

A duck, my lads,
laid
in waddling clothes
miles from the sea
months from the water.

Avast there! Wandering
the sunset plank
like a drunk.

The sun has got his balaclava on
back to front.

★

My dear sons.
Christmas like this
brings on the big sobs.

Boys, I'm sorry.
I should be a better father,
make you laugh.

Watch this card trick: you
take a card, any card. You
memorise it and then.

I forget. I have the deck
in front of me and I forget!

I'm sorry. Night pulls
the teeth of day;
I'm not a monster, boys.
I'm a poetry.

★

He's got me covered. Listen:
"Love poem. Her eyes
were like three crows in a cornfield
and when she spoke it was like
three crows in a cornfield.
She undressed, and three crows
squatted in a cornfield."

He's bound me hand and foot,
the Doctor Frankenstein,
stitched me to myself.

65

Lads I'm not a monster
I'm a secondhand tent.

Night pulls the teeth of day
scatters them over the sky
like three crows in a cornfield.

I finished the love story
lines ago in the white.

Lads I am your affectionate father
who is not a monster but a poetry.

★

You are too young to understand,
my children.

I'm a nut, fellers.
I'm Phil O'Sparks
the Tortured Torso;
I'm slipping away.

I've been beaten on the soles of my feet
repeatedly for three months
with a heavy concrete floor
and I am still nowhere,

miles away across the black
woods and the white walls.

"I ate twelve moths
in a year, sizzling
in the mouth's flame"

(Not a monster but a poetry!)

I have been deprived of sleep
for sixty-five days
and my dreams are queueing up
behind the cell door.
A guard is busking
up and down the line
with tap shoes and a violin

and my dreams
are turning their curved faces to the wall.

★

I hope you are saving these letters
sons of mine

for Volume Four: "The Prison Letters
of Frankenstein's Unfortunate Mistake
who did not break under torture or
if he did he had his attention distracted
while they stitched him back together
to face more machines."

The title is long winded.
But then so is life.

Children. I am not even a poetry.
I am a philosoph.

★

Last night they bound and gagged me.
They rammed a voice into my ear
and they crooned that this
is to be my last letter.
They are holding my broken paws as I type.

I am muter than mute. As mute
as mute can be. Bloody mute.

Last night
they deprived me of my head
for sixty five days

and tied a starving prisoner
across my stomach
so that I could not dream.

A duck, my lads,
lying in weeds
miles from the land
months from the forest.

Closing the sunset gap
like a mouth

closed for the night.

## Sessions

### 1.

It started with the telephone
ringing ringing
as I threw the baby down
(she bounced)
tripped over the push chair
(I bounced)
put my foot through the telly
(It's rented)
and I got there.

And it stopped.
And I turned.
And it started.
And I turned.
and I grabbed the mouthpiece

and a voice said
          "Ian McWilliams?"
and I said

          "No but I could be"

and the voice said

          "I'm running a little festival"

          "Oh yes" I said.

          "At my little school in Thurton-on-the-Marsh"

          "Oh yes" I said.

          "I've got a mime artist. At least
          I think I have.
          He never answers the phone"

          "Oh yes"

          "I've got a theatre group.
          They're doing Shakespeare.
          Macbeth. Do you know Macbeth?"

          "Oh yes"

          "They're doing it in Eskimo Dress.
          Three witches as polar bears"

          "Oh yes"

"And I thought
well I thought
yes I thought
I ought to have
some poetry."

She pronounced it Poyertroy.

"Oh yes"

"I wrote to Faber.
And Faber.
They were both out.
But a really nice man
agreed to send a blow up doll
of Ted Hughes"

"Oh yes"

"And then I tried
to get some other poets
I tried
Roger McGough
Adrian Henri
Adrian Mitchell
Adrian Adrian
and finally
I got through
to you."

"Oh yes."

"Will you do it?
Will you do it?
I can pay you £40.00
plus travel.

Will you do it?"

"Okay.
I'll do it."

"Good. I've sorted out some trains.
You leave Barnsley at 0408
and you get to our school
just an hour before we start.

I'm so glad you can do it."

2.

The drunk
on the 5.am train
is poking his slopbucket breath
into my face.

"Now then pal,
what's your line of work?"

I stare into his eyes,
see the same face
I saw in the mirror
at four o'clock.

Normally I don't tell them.
Today I say
"I'm a poet."

The drunk
on the 5.am train
is poking his slopbucket breath
into my face.

"Poet? I know a poem:
Miranda dear Miranda
I love your little bum
specially when you sit it
on my big fat tum"

The train stops.
All the sleepy passengers
are staring at me.

And as he repeats the poem
twice, three times
I feel my ticket
burn away in my pocket.


3.

Mr. McErrrr
I'd like you to meet Mr. Thrust;
He's a taxidermist-in-schools.
Mr. Thrust, Mr. McErrrr
He stuffs things, yes, for a living...
Isn't that amazing Mr.....
We've read about these people who stuff things
and here's one in the flesh.
As it were.

What's in his bag?
You may well ask.
It's his badger.
It was flattened by a tractor.

He's going to stuff it
in lessons three and four
for a group of slow learners
in a temporary classroom

and we thought that
as he stuffed it
you could improvise a poem
like the troubadours used to.

You can do it Mr. Mc
You can do it.
I know you can.
You can do it.

4.

"Children... (I haven't told them you're coming. It's a surprise!
They *hate* poetry!)... Children... this gentleman is Mr., er, and
do you know what he does? No Darren, he isn't a pervert. No,
Tracy, he isn't a gorilla in a suit. No, he's a poet. He's had several
books published. He's been on Radio 3. He's met Peter Redgrove!
He's going to read you some of his poems, and then maybe get
you to write some. Isn't that exciting? Isn't it? Isn't it?"

## *Pushing, May 1984*

Kate's pink bonnet bobs
as she points to a flower.

I wheel her pushchair forward
she leans over to the colours.

Last time I brought her here
she was only two months old

and she never made a sound.
This time she shouts and points.

A tree moves, a car moves,
a striking pitman picks coal

shuffling the dirt, his dark head
bobbing. When we get back home

she won't have any words
to tell her mother what we saw

but she'll try. She starts to cry,
she always does when I turn her round

to push her back, her finger pointing.


## *Coalpicking, Broomhill*

We are bending over
like men after shellfish.
We dart like birds
in the hard November sun.
I have left the riddle
by a frozen puddle
and we are digging.

The field is turned over,
riddled, left to freeze;
there is nothing here.
A dozen police vans
rumble down the road
towards Cortonwood.
A man throws his shovel
on the stiff ground,
the harsh wind clutches us.
We say nothing,

yet still my daughter
insists on waking at four
in clenched blue darkness

and downstairs we build
on the floor before dawn
using bricks, people, books, anything.

# Visitors: Armthorpe, August 1984

Four of them, sitting in the kitchen
drinking tea, I imagine saucers.
I am probably wrong about the saucers.
A hot August day in the kitchen.

*"The back door was unlocked*
*but they kicked it in.*
*Police said 'Send the bastards out'*
*then the policeman jammed the door*

*into my face".* I imagine a kitchen,
I am probably wrong about the saucers.
I imagine heartbroken saucers
with patterns of flowers.

# The Curious Visitors: Buxton, June 1986

"A curious visitor to Buxton in 1790 would have encountered unusual
activity near the Goslin Boat tollgate. From the mouth of a nearby tunnel,
a boat laden with coal appeared from time to time, to be unloaded and
returned into the darkness, propelled by a boy of about twelve."
— *The Coalmines of Buxton* by A.F. Roberts and J.R. Leach

From Chest, Cap Sitch, Gold Sitch, Goyt Moss,
Latch, Whatshaw, Dane Head, Mouse Trap,

Abraham Goodwin is tunnelling upward,
William Street is digging

and the curious visitors
are applauding themselves.

When the applause stops
they will hear the sound

of a gate being closed
for the last time.

So the applause won't stop,
the applause keeps going.

William Street keeps digging.
John Price is digging.

John Price walked from Devon
to work in the Buxton mines.

If the applause would stop
they would hear his feet

so the applause won't stop.
"In times of national emergency

the mines were reopened
for brief periods."

Open them now:
close the applause.

Lock it in Chest,
Shut it in Latch,

"unloaded and returned
into the darkness".


## Propp's Last Case

"Occasionally, during the late '50s and early '60s, the dominant position
of the realist Yorkshire novel was challenged by a number of American-
influenced works known as the *hardboiled* school of Yorkshire prose."
– McMillan, *Trends in't Yorkshire Novel*, unpublished.

It was unthinkable midnight or Autumn
in a blackish Barnsley of the mind.

My helmet hung on her hatstand,
the beam pointing straight up, white.
She was kissing me
like they kiss on radio plays:

noisily.

It was coaldark midnight or Autumn:
I guess the two are interchangeable.

I tried to shine but my lamp went out
and I'd left my batteries with the safety man.
She was still kissing me
like they do on radio plays:

I couldn't breathe.

"You're smothering me," I said.
"Baby, I've got the dust," she purred,
"you just put it on the shovel
and you snort it up."

Then the room felt like Autumn or midnight
and I didn't care. I was breathing
like they breathe on radio plays,

it was the end of something. I wanted out.
"Midnight or Autumn?" she asked,
and I thought she meant her lingerie.

She meant her dogs.

As they chased me I tried to make a joke
about not being able to run properly
but my mouth was full of midnight
or Autumn and she was laughing like they laugh
on radio plays and I was gasping like they gasp
just before they die
on radio plays.

# Action

The books get smaller and smaller
until
there is only the one small book

and it is not in their hands.
And they will be punished
because the one small book
is not in their hands

as though
it is their fault

and you are using their lives
to save their lives.

Manchester, November.
Terrible rain over Beswick.
Two children huddle
in the closed doorway of a school
eating a tiny pork pie.

The open doors
get smaller and smaller
until
there is only the one small door

and it is not in their hands, so

use their lives
save their lives
win.

## Poem (Poem) and PS (Draft)

Just this; the babby with her dad's cap
covering her head like a halo

and the dad, taking the cap off her head,
bending his own head to put it on

and the ache in the movement
of that bending head

and the babby reaching for the cap
that will fit her soon enough.

PS:     So to clear the poem
        from his head he takes

        So to brush that poem
        right out of his hair

        He goes for a walk
        sees two teams playing football
        the poem is still washing

        the poem is still waving
        around in his head
        so he looks for caps but all he sees
        are shirts and shorts.

        Green shirts, blue shorts,
        noise of the two sides
        rubbing each other's space.

        Blue shirts, yellow shorts
        noise of the two sides
        taking each other's space.

His head is not clear.
The cap is still in it.

The poem with the cap
is still in it.


# From An Evening With The Model Of "The Venus and the Shaving Brushes"

1.  I was sitting on my usual stool.
    She walked into the bar.
    I heard a faint hissing noise.

2.  She glanced over the lights of the city.
    "I am full of shaving brushes
    so people think I am a shaving brush,"
    she said. I did not understand.

3.  "Sometimes I go to the Tate and I see her;
    she looks more like me than I do,
    as is the way with the exploited."

4.  She screamed and would not
    go near the bathroom.

5.  "If I touch myself
    I can feel only
    the soft parts of the brushes
    and the hard parts of the brushes.
    This is what he has done to me."

6.  "How wide he had
    to force my mouth
    you will never know.
    I had no time to swallow."

7.  In the morning she arched over my bed
    coughing and spitting up lengths of horsehair.
    "It gets worse as the years pass," she said.

8.  I said that I could hear the birds singing.
    She looked at me with a face full of pity
    as though it was not important
    to hear the birds singing.

9.  "I am in someone else's image
    and that is the worst thing of all."

## *Move*

You smiled,
said I'd built it
and that was why
it was falling apart.

So the fat removal man
and the thin removal man
carried the creaky white wardrobe
out,

left the room
holding only us

and the furniture
we will always have:

creaky, home made,
one only, made to measure,
built to last, not a toy,

actual size.

## The Photographer's Subject

found himself
framed in the brightness of windows,

saw lights in the sky
and lights in doorways,

stood very still
for a few seconds

and flattened
into grey.


## Just the Facts, Just the

In the play room
Dean won't eat his cabbage.
His mother whispers to him,
"Look, I know you don't like cabbage..."
His dad, who has been exchanging shy smiles
with me all weekend, says,
"Tha dun't like cabbage, all reight,
tha dun't..."

We sit around on the small chairs,
encouraging. Enormous toys
line the walls like prefects,
two huge snails lick themselves
up the side of the glass case,
thirty seven fish move in a tank.

We are on the eighth floor. Six
floors down, my mother settles
herself painfully into a new hip.

On the eighth floor, my daughter
spoons mush into her mouth. Tonight
the doctor will tell her to go home.
I close my eyes and see her jerking
about on the settee, bright red,
making little cardboard cries.

Cardboard cries? Pull together yourself.
Just the facts, just the

Late at night, driving between Barnburgh
and Goldthorpe, a couple making love
in a ditch, caught in the light of the
car lights, looking like a brightly
coloured bird or a brightly coloured
animal.

Yes, I guess
you are right.
Any facts
will do.

## Simple Story

Getting ready for the bath
I shake money
from my trousers to the bedroom floor.

Kate lies on the floor
saying, "No, no," in a voice
quiet as the shut curtains.

I pull back the curtains,
knock the window wide.
We fold up the quilt,

soak the stinking quilt
in the bath. Kate sleeps
peacefully in our big bed.

Walking over to the bed
I feel two cool coins
sticking to my feet


## Man in Hotel Room with Stolen Fork

The taxis circle
round the square
taking people from places
to places.

It's mid-December in WC1.
The day is over, the bulb lingers on.
*Man in hotel fork with stolen room.*

He stole the fork in a curry place,
now there's guilt written sweaty all over his face.
*Man in stolen hotel room with fork.*

In the hallway it's Christmas, on the stairs it's goodwill
as he forks in the meat and it makes him feel ill.
*Man in stolen fork with hotel room.*

He's sick in the basin, he's sick in the bin.
He's empty as history, lonely as sin.
*Room in stolen man with hotel fork.*

And the taxis circle
round the square
taking people from places
to places.

## Against Realism

At the poetry workshop
the woman holds up a plum.

"Can I read this poem about a plum?"
she says.

"That is a very well written poem
about a plum," I say.

"It is a plum!"
someone shouts.

"It is certainly very fine writing."
I reply, wittily.


## Some Poetry Presses I Will Certainly Set Up
in the Next Three Weeks

Go to your Room! Press
What the Fat Man did Next Press
This is a Joke Press

24 pages
perfect bound

Don't Tell Me Press
The Isle of Man is Made Out of Cheese Press
The Tap Room of the New Station Inn Press

32 pages
perfect bound

The Expensive Press
The Ted Hughes is Two Men in a Suit Press
The Press Here Press

48 pages
perfect bound

## Landing Practice

Just carry on sleeping;
don't think about the moment

when the helicopter came very close
and I picked you up and carried you

along the beach. Don't wake up.
Don't think about the mole

that I told you was asleep,
and we never saw it flying

but when we came back it had gone
and the helicopter was a word

at the edge of the sky's page.
"The sleeping mole flew away,"

you said. I nodded. I nodded.
*I hate helicopters*, I said,

*all helicopters*. When
I picked you up and carried you

along the beach, crying,
for a second I was all the scared people,

and a dead mole flew over my head
into the sea.


## The Prince of Wales visits Alnwick
*(from a photograph)*

The prince is a blur in his fast car.
A hand waves from a thin crowd.

There is a man in knickerbockers.
There are two women leaning from windows.

There are two men at the cobbler's door.
There is a mend up the middle

where the photograph has been torn.
There is a single word behind the head

of the speeding prince: Simpson,
a shop-sign in the grey background

like a bullet with his name on it.


## Cracking Icicles in Totley Tunnel

Into the dark tunnel
from the white hills
the train slows, almost
stops.

Across the aisle
a man cups his eyes
against the dark window.

I do the same. Peer.
Ice. Heavy, almost marble, solid, almost
alive ice.
Cracking and rumbling on the roof.

But we are regular travellers
and we are used to such warnings
in the dark tunnel
under the white
and constant hills

the train slows, almost
stops, then

begins to go faster
as the ice is gone
at the end of resistance
we rush into darkness

like a van
speeding from
a fenced-in printworks,

like a fenced-in bus
speeding from a pit.

## Tall in the Saddle

Just remember

when they crash through the streets
of a village with a name
you cannot pronounce

and when they crash through the streets
of a village with a name
you can pronounce

and when they crash through the streets
you know like the back of your house

the horse may be tall,
the saddle may be tall,
the stick may be tall,

but the man in the saddle is not tall,
    the man in the saddle is not tall.

# POETRY
## *Signatures*

Gillian Clarke, *Selected Poems*                                        0 85635 594 1
'. . . record the changes economic collapse is bringing to Wales, memories
of a journey through France, fruit, flowers and work in the fields. . . . the
poems are richly satisfying, accumulating like bottled fruit gleaming
along a pantry shelf.' – *Stand*

Donald Davie, *Selected Poems*                                        0 85635 595 X
'Davie is an exciting poet because he takes nothing for granted, and
because he takes risks . . . making sense and making whole, as and
wherever he can.' – *Guardian*

A.D. Hope, *Selected Poems*                                        0 85635 640 9
'The first Australian to make a name outside his homeland, Hope is one
of the finest poets writing in English . . . this well-made selection shows
Hope pursuing truth and reason in the richest and most resonant lan-
guage.' – *Observer*

Elizabeth Jennings, *Selected Poems*                                        0 85635 282 9
'She conveys a sense of something hidden but powerfully alive in her;
she may be the last poet of what used to be called the soul. . . . She is
one of the few living poets one could not do without.' – *Spectator*

Ian McMillan, *Selected Poems*                                        0 85635 718 9
'. . . are poems of their time; they share a cool obliquity with Elvis Cos-
tello's songs, Glen Baxter's cartoons . . . but they do not pander to their
time, . . . exploiting language's ambiguous malfunctions and unexpected
local quirks.' – *Times Literary Supplement*

Edwin Morgan, *Selected Poems*                                        0 85635 596 8
'. . . combine verbal inventiveness and formal innovation . . . at the same
time he luminously communicates the power and delight of the ordi-
nary.' – *Times Literary Supplement*

Les A. Murray, *Selected Poems*                                        0 85635 667 0
'Les A. Murray is an Australian, a waterfall of a poet, satisfying as a
draught of Coonawarra Cabernet – a year's discovery.' – *Guardian*

Iain Crichton Smith, *Selected Poems*                    0 85635 597 6
'...an indubitably inspired poet, taking on the world in poem after poem.' – *The Times*

Jeffrey Wainwright, *Selected Poems*                    0 85635 598 4
'...his uncanny ability to voice the feelings of the oppressed and dissenting and thus to range from...domestic intimacy to visionary fervour has already made his historical cycles minor classics.' – *Sunday Times*

Sylvia Townsend Warner, *Selected Poems*                    0 85635 585 2
'Anyone thinking that wit, penetration...an enduring and exact delight in the natural world, all united with absolute integrity, are as needed as they are rare, would do well to read [Sylvia Townsend Warner's poems].' – *Observer*

Andrew Waterman, *Selected Poems*                    0 85635 668 8
'...a highly intelligent poet [who lectures at the New University of Ulster] for whom the troubles are, in every sense, on the doorstep, and his *Selected Poems* is an impressive volume.' – *Encounter*

Robert Wells, *Selected Poems*                    0 85635 669 7
'He is a scholar familiar with Virgil and Theocritus; he has also worked as a farm hand...his acute sense of physical presence extends at once to areas at once physiological and psychological...He is undoubtedly a poet.' – *London Review of Books*

# Fyfield*Books*

"The Fyfield Books series provides an admirable service in publishing good inexpensive selections from the works of interesting but neglected poets"
– *British Book News*

THOMAS LOVELL BEDDOES (1803-49)
Selected Poems
*edited by Judith Higgens*

THE BRONTË SISTERS
Selected Poems
*edited by Stevie Davies*

ELIZABETH BARRETT BROWNING (1806-61)
Selected Poems
*edited by Malcolm Hicks*

THOMAS CAMPION (1567-1620)
Ayres and Observations
*edited by Joan Hart*

GEORGE CHAPMAN (?1559-1634)
Selected Poems
*edited by Eirean Wain*

THOMAS CHATTERTON (1752-70)
Selected Poems
*edited by Grevel Lindop*

CHARLES COTTON (1630-87)
Selected Poems
*edited by Ken Robinson*

WILLIAM COWPER (1731-1800)
Selected Poems
*edited by Nick Rhodes*

GEORGE CRABBE (1754-1832)
Selected Poems
*edited by Jem Poster*

RICHARD CRASHAW (1612/13-49)
Selected Poems
*edited by Michael Cayley*

MICHAEL DRAYTON (1563-1631)
Selected Poems
*edited by Vivian Thomas*

GEORGE GASCOIGNE (1530-77)
The Green Knight:
selected poems and prose
*edited by Roger Pooley*

JOHN GAY (1685-1732)
Selected Poems
*edited by Marcus Walsh*

JOHN GOWER (1330-1408)
Selected Poetry
*edited by Carole Weinberg*

THOMAS GRAY (1716-71)
Selected Poems
*edited by John Heath-Stubbs*

ROBERT HENRYSON (1425?-1508?)
Selected Poems
*edited by W.R.J. Barron*

ROBERT HERRICK (1591-1674)
Selected Poems
*edited by David Jesson-Dibley*

THOMAS HOCCLEVE (?1348-1430)
Selected Poems
*edited by Bernard O'Donoghue*

BEN JONSON (1572-1637)
Epigrams & The Forest
*edited by Richard Dutton*

WALTER SAVAGE LANDOR (1775-1864)
Selected Poems and Prose
*edited by Keith Hanley*

ANDREW MARVELL (1621-78)
Selected Poems
*edited by Bill Hutchings*

GEORGE MEREDITH (1828-1909)
Selected Poems
*edited by Keith Hanley*

CHARLES OF ORLEANS (1394-1465)
Selected Poems
*edited by Sally Purcell*

SIR WALTER RALEGH (?1554-1618)
Selected Writings
*edited by Gerald Hammond*

JOHN WILMOT, EARL OF ROCHESTER
(1648-80)
The Debt to Pleasure
*edited by John Adlard*

CHRISTINA ROSSETTI (1830-94)
Selected Poems
*edited by C.H. Sisson*

SIR PHILIP SIDNEY (1554-86)
Selected Poetry and Prose
*edited by Richard Dutton*

JOHN SKELTON (1460-1529)
Selected Poems
*edited by Gerald Hammond*

CHRISTOPHER SMART (1722-71)
Selected Poems
*edited by Marcus Walsh*

DONALD STANFORD (editor)
Three Poets of the Rhymers' Club:
Lionel Johnson, Ernest Dowson,
John Davidson

HENRY HOWARD, EARL OF SURREY
(1517-47)
Selected Poems
*edited by Dennis Keene*

JONATHAN SWIFT (1667-1745)
Selected Poems
*edited by C.H. Sisson*

ALGERNON CHARLES SWINBURNE
(1837-1909)
Selected Poems
*edited by L.M. Findlay*

ARTHUR SYMONS (1865-1945)
Selected Writings
*edited by R.V. Holdsworth*

THOMAS TRAHERNE (?1637-74)
Selected Writings
*edited by Dick Davis*

HENRY VAUGHAN (1622-95)
Selected Poems
*edited by Robert B. Shaw*

ANNE FINCH, COUNTESS OF WINCHILSEA
(1661-1720)
Selected Poems
*edited by Denys Thompson*

EDWARD YOUNG (1683-1765)
Selected Poems
*edited by Brian Hepworth*

"Carcanet are doing an excellent job in this series: the editions are labours of love, not just commercial enterprises. I hope they are familiar to all readers and teachers of literature." – *Times Literary Supplement*